JOURNEY
OF A
LIFT COMPANY

7 Powerful Ways your LIFT Business can make you Invincible

7 Powerful Ways your LIFT Business can make you Invincible

By

HARSH GUPTA

Published Internationally by

PENDOWN PRESS

***Powered by* Gullybaba Publishing House Pvt. Ltd.,**
An ISO 9001 & ISO 14001 Certified Co.,
Regd. Office: 2525/193, 1st Floor, Onkar Nagar-A, Tri Nagar, Delhi-110035
Ph.: 09350849407, 09312235086
E-mail: info@pendownpress.com
Branch Office: 1A/2A, 20, Hari Sadan, Ansari Road, Daryaganj, New Delhi-110002
Ph.: 011-45794768
Website: PendownPress.com

First Edition: 2020

ISBN: 978-93-90557-24-0

Layout Design: Pendown Press Publishing

CONTENTS

INTRODUCTION

Hello, my name is Harsh Gupta. I am an elevator Mechanical Design Consultant.

My Journey with the custom-based elevator design began 6 years back when I first customized a lift for one of the leading player of the market.

I was astonished to see how a customized product can put you in a separate league compared to your competitors.

Over 6 years, we have helped more than 100 lift companies to deliver a customized solution to their customers, which has proven to be the most effective way for my top-ranking customers to get more business and maintain their leadership.

I am sharing this e-book, so that lot of lift companies who made a bold decision in their life by leaving behind their day job to start their own company, can finally live their passion.

It pains me when I see an entrepreneur who started their own company with so much passion, ends up in a loop of hopelessness and distrust, only because of some common myths. I want to make sure, that those same entrepreneurs can expand their business and create a unique identity.

So, let us look into the mistakes you can avoid in your journey.

Your well-wisher

–Harsh Gupta

CHAPTER 1

UNDERSTAND THE NEED-DO NOT RUSH TO SELL

The first mistake that everyone makes is to rush into selling and starts rambling about the products they offer, such as the extra features that they are installing, what are their competitors lacking, etc.

"You need to stop right there
and understand the need
of your customers."

For instance

(1) Purpose of the lift–Goods Lift, Passenger Lift or Both

(2) Age groups of people who are going to use the lift

(3) Type of usage of the lift

(4) Frequency of the lift going to get used

(5) Number of people utilizing the lift

(6) The installation location of the lift

We need to understand these needs, because in our past experiences, there are lots of dissatisfied customers even after final handover of the product.

One of such study is as below:

"The place of installation was a grocery retail store, the lift was being man-handled and there was a lot of up-down of grocery items like Rice, Pulses, Oil, Flour, etc., resulting in irreparable damage and reduced lift life and need for regular maintenance. There was lot of inconvenience due to breakdown on regular working days. The problem observed was that items were getting stuck in the "aluminium sill" of doors and due to continuous use of trolley, the panels were "out of shape".

Therefore, we had to re-design Scratch-Proof Panels for the Car Cabin with "groove-less sill doors" and we used plain doors instead of vision panels due to its usage type."

Another example would be, if old-age passengers are using the facility, then we need vision panel doors with width enough for a wheelchair to enter. In this scenario, we will use low-speed machines and invest in the intercom facility for an emergency.

Therefore, it is very essential to understand the entire need before actually selling your product.

CHAPTER 2

GET IN THE CLIENT'S SEAT–BE THE CLIENT YOU WANT TO SELL

Has it ever happened with you, that your order is booked by your competitors by offering an inferior product than yours? If the answer is yes, then you must have tried to provide your best flagship lift design with a lot of new technology without analyzing the real need.

The second mistake is

"We sell what we feel is right for our customers, not what our customer thinks is right."

You have to create a solution as per the mindset of future lift owner, which is possible only by asking questions. For example, you need to know,

- Whether your customer is interested in High-end designer product or an economical design?
- Whether your customer's priority is Quality or Pricing?
- Whether it is for personal use or further renting out?
- Is your customer interested in availing AMC or not?

For instance

"A real-estate developer in the line of developing budgeted flats or houses may get a Uniquely Designed Lift for their own personal use and might prefer an

Economic Classic Standard lift for their housing projects."

"Likewise, where an architect or an interior designer is involved with your customer, they might suggest a designer car, in an attempt to match their design pallet with the lift interiors."

To successfully sell, we need a personalized design for every new customer, because at last your customer is human and every human has different priorities and preferences.

CHAPTER 3

DO NOT VOMIT- PRESENT THE MOST VIABLE PRODUCT

Many times, after interviewing your customers and understanding their mindset, you tend to offer many solutions to show variety or just to simply impress.

If you offer too many options, then it completely defeats the purpose of the study that you did in the first place for your prospect.

Next thing you know is that "Customer is Confused" and your potential customer's final reply will be "I will get back to you."

"For example: You visit a retail store for buying clothes and the salesman starts showing you clothes of various colors and designs. You are being showed clothes for casual wear, office wear, smart casuals and all other types available at the store.

On the other hand, you are being asked your color preferences, or your preference for plain shirt or a printed, are you purchasing for your own or for gifting to someone, what is the occasion you have to dress up for, *i.e.*, you need for your regular office wear or for a birthday party. After all these questions, the salesman shows you some options as per your answers."

Which experience would be better for you?

Exactly!! The second one!

To avoid the first situation, you must provide ONE perfect solution.

You have to demonstrate to your customer the research you have done and the reason why it is the perfect product requirement according to the need of the hour.

Everything else that anyone offers will not hold any stand in front of your tailor-made design.

CHAPTER 4

AVOID TECHNICAL JARGON-SIMPLIFY YOUR PITCH/ PROPOSAL

Most of the time, to prove our credibility to the customer, we use a lot of technical terms in the process of explaining our product instead of how our product solves their problems.

Your customer does not care about the technology, the only concern of your customer is, how your design solves their problem and how your piece of technology helps them complete their kit of needs.

Instead follow these 5 simple steps as below:

- Use very simple terms at the time of explaining.
- Search for layman terms as an alternate to technical language, when you are explaining some specific features.
- Try to highlight safety points of your product in simple terms.
- Try to relate the technology with simple relatable equipment that we use in our day-to-day life.
- The most important-Keep the line of conversation as ingenious as possible to make your customer feel more educated and informed.

A customer is more comfortable in making a purchase, if he thinks he understands the technology rather than, when it sounds too complicated to understand.

"ALWAYS USE LAYMAN TERMS IN YOUR EXPLANATION"

5 CHAPTER

QUESTION EVERYTHING–ASK YOUR CLIENT THEIR BIGGEST CONCERN

This tip is the biggest game-changer. It can help you get premium orders with no competition.

Every customer has a lot of concerns in the process of choosing their lift partner. Most of the time, everyone seems to take care of their 80% problems in one way or the other.

Even after that, the final order is given to the one who solves only the remaining 20% problem.

You have to specifically ask your customer, what is the deciding factor for them in choosing the right lift partner. You have to solve the query which holds the most value for your customer to side-line-competitors, even MNCs, in the eyes of your customer.

The pain-points of the end-user can be anything like

- The budget is too low
- The installation time is too long
- The desired solution is not satisfactory
- Safety of the lift is not up to the mark
- The response time is too late

There can be similar concerns of your customers that need to be addressed.

In a nutshell, your entire sales pitch gets compressed into a little task of highlighting the pain-points, in order to showcase the "Perfect Solution"

CHAPTER 6

USE SNIPER TECHNIQUE–BE PRECISE IN YOUR PROPOSAL

Now, you have already studied your customer to its full potential and now is the time to use it.

Once you have assembled all the data, you will have to start preparing a final proposal.

"One should be very clear on what they are proposing"

You should have a mental clear visualization of these "9" crucial points:

- The lift design and its parameters
- The brands you are planning to use
- The capacity you are will be using
- The source of the raw materials
- The booking amount percentage required
- The Team Members you need to deploy
- The Alternate options in contingency cases
- The Month-Wise Completion Plan
- The exact lead-time to deliver

Once you have conceptualized these nine points,your final proposal will have clarity in it with all the definite answers. It reflects your way of working style. The customers will be able to see your accuracy instead of the competitor's clutter.

A sharply created proposal eliminates deviation of customer's focus to non-relevant areas. Also, it makes it easier for you to focus on "The One Proposal", rather than wasting time on preparing multiple proposals after every discussion.

7 CHAPTER

MOST IMPORTANT- TAKE FEEDBACK ON YOUR OFFER

"Has it ever happened, that after explaining your product and its features, you send a proposal to your customer and you never heard back from them OR you end up in an endless discussion of negotiation?"

If your answer is yes (or yes), then you are missing just one step to overcome such situations.

The key is to take feedback on the solution offered on the basis of your discussions with the prospect. It enlightens the customer the efforts you have put in, to provide the best possible solution. Also, it sharpens your skills in understanding and developing customised offers.

The feedback helps you fill the gaps in the final study of your prospect's need. It is the best chance for you to create the PERFECT proposal and get the business started on your terms.

Henceforth, please make sure to take feedback from your customer before quoting the final price.

CHAPTER 8

HOW TO USE THIS MINI BOOK

As the author of this Instabook, I have tried my level best to incorporate all the things that are worth knowing for my readers who are in lift business. And when there is the quest to cater all, you cannot specify as to who wants what. But, the Beauty of reading a Book is of course to know what you want to know, as well as what others want to know. And this indeed gives us a sense of collective readership. A book happens to be for one and all.

When I started creating Content List, I kept into consideration all the essential elements in a lift business. You may already be aware and a practitioner of one or more of the headings mentioned in the Content List. Though I am sure that this InstaBook will add to your knowledge, even if you already know lots of things about a particular topic, I would like to advise you that to start with you may select a topic you think, is the most valuable for you as a student of lift business.

When you get satisfied with the knowledge provided here, you will yourself become radioactive to read other chapters as well and implement it in your modus operandi. Simply put, here it is not incumbent on you to finish chapter one and then only you will get the key to open chapter two. When you move freely, you cover all places!

CALL TO ACTION

I have shared with you my valuable lessons that I have learned after working with numerous lift companies.

The basic principle always remains the same. It is upon you, how you want it for yourself. You want to take the best out of it and achieve greatness out of it or whether you want to be stuck to the mediocrity you are facing.

I appeal you to take the charge and make the change. I am available to support you. You can either do it all by yourself or take an expert advice.

For any kind of support, mail us at INFO@JBGEPL.COM or enquire for a 1 to 1 Zoom Session.

www.ingramcontent.com/pod-product-compliance
Ingram Content Group UK Ltd.
Pitfield, Milton Keynes, MK11 3LW, UK
UKHW020843020826
14060UKWH00022B/20